THE VICTORIAN STEAMPUNK TAROT

UNRAVEL THE MYSTERIES OF THE PAST, PRESENT, AND FUTURE

LIZ DEAN

ILLUSTRATED BY BEV SPEIGHT

CICO BOOKS
LONDON NEW YORK

Liz: *I personally dedicate this book to MWY and my mentor in spirit, the late Jonathan Dee.*

Bev: *I would like to dedicate this book to my lovely circle–David, Archie, Mum, Cath, Alfie, and Eian.*

Published in 2014 by CICO Books
An imprint of Ryland Peters & Small
20–21 Jockey's Fields   341E 116th Street
London WC1R 4BW   New York, NY 10029

10 9 8 7

Conceived by Liz Dean and Bev Speight

Text © Liz Dean 2014
Design and illustration © CICO Books 2014

ILLUSTRATOR: BEV SPEIGHT
DESIGNER: PAUL TILBY
EDITOR: JUDY BARRATT

The author's moral rights have been asserted. All rights reserved. No part of this publication may be reproduced, stored in a retrieval system, or transmitted in any form or by any means, electronic, mechanical, photocopying, or otherwise, without the prior permission of the publisher.

A CIP catalog record for this book is available from the Library of Congress and the British Library.

ISBN 978 1 78249 111 8

Printed in China

Many thanks to Cindy Richards, Lauren Mulholland, Paul Tilby, and all at CICO Books. Thanks also to our agent, Chelsey Fox.

MIX
Paper from responsible sources
FSC® C106563

CONTENTS

INTRODUCING THE STEAMPUNK TAROT 4-5

LAYING THE CARDS

BEFORE YOU BEGIN 6

PAST, PRESENT, AND FUTURE 7

SPIRIT MESSAGES 8

ASK THREE TIMES 9

TO ANSWER A QUESTION 10

WEEK AHEAD AND YEAR AHEAD 11

THE CROSS 12

THE CARDS AND THEIR MEANINGS

13 THE MAJOR ARCANA

36 THE MINOR ARCANA

37 THE SUIT OF DRAGONFLIES

44 THE SUIT OF MOTHS

51 THE SUIT OF BEES

58 THE SUIT OF BEETLES

INTRODUCING THE STEAMPUNK TAROT

Steampunk is the fusion of Victorian invention (the "steam" that powered the nineteenth-century industrial world) and the spirit of counterculture (the "punk"). It is vintage combined with science fiction in worlds where anything is possible: clockwork butterflies merge with plasma screens, hot-air balloons sweep over fantasy landscapes in a realm in which the past and the future are constantly reinvented. Expressed in art, literature, fashion, and film, steampunk is inspired by writers such as Jules Verne, Mary Shelley, and Edgar Allan Poe, and by themes as diverse as burlesque, alternative histories, and mechanical engineering. Modern-day movies such as *Sherlock Holmes* and *The League of Extraordinary Gentlemen* showcase some elements of the ever-evolving steampunk look.

As a movement, steampunk is considered a branch of cyberpunk, a science-fiction genre of apocalyptic high tech (think *The Terminator*). Science-fiction writer K.W. Jeter first coined the term "steampunk" in 1987 to describe his novel *Morlock Night* and novels by Tim Powers and James Blaylock, all of which share a Victorian setting. Also on the cyberpunk family tree is "dieselpunk," which takes its inspiration from the years 1920 to 1940 (the *Indiana Jones* era), and "gaslight romance," a subset of steampunk that has been applied to Victorian novels with less focus on science—such as those of *Dracula* creator Bram Stoker.

INTRODUCING THE STEAMPUNK TAROT

THE TAROT CONNECTION

The worlds of steampunk and tarot are well suited. Famed for subversion, both steampunk and tarot rely upon continual reinvention, transcending eras, and pioneering new perspectives. For the past 600 years, artists and writers have adapted the tarot's core symbols—its archetypes—to create new interpretations that continue to resonate with our instinctual selves.

Every tarot deck contains archetypes—characters such as The Fool, The Hermit, and The Lovers, as well as personifications of the virtues Justice, Temperance, and Strength. Recast over the centuries, these archetypes represent how tarot imagery has changed in line with our own tastes and preoccupations—from quantum physics through vampires, angels through fairy tales.

In *The Steampunk Tarot*, inspiration comes from the spiritualist movement that began in the UK and the USA in the 1840s, at the beginning of Queen Victoria's reign, along with the Rider Waite and Visconti-Sforza tarot symbolism. The "punk" is the tarot itself—the process of shuffling the cards and laying them out, juxtaposing the cards and their symbols before telling a story. The practice of tarot reading leads us to other worlds and other possibilities and opens up our imagination and intuition. Just like steampunk, tarot cards show us the past, present, and future, and a world of magical possibilities.

THE CARDS

The 78 cards follow the standard tarot structure, with 22 major arcana (or trump) cards, and 56 minor arcana cards arranged in four suits of 14 cards each. The minor arcana suits relate to the traditional elements that represent the suits of classic tarot decks. However, new suit symbols express the Victorian obsession with botanical collections and the natural world.

SUIT	TRADITIONAL	ELEMENT
DRAGONFLIES	CUPS	WATER
MOTHS	WANDS	FIRE
BEES	SWORDS	AIR
BEETLES	PENTACLES/COINS	EARTH

LAYING THE CARDS

BEFORE YOU BEGIN

CREATING A SPACE

Conduct your reading in a peaceful space where you feel relaxed and comfortable. Find a flat, clean surface on which to lay your cards. You might like to practice a short ritual before you lay out the cards—rituals help quieten the chatter of the mind and amplify intuition. For example, before each reading you might light a candle, close your eyes, and take a few calming breaths.

USING THE CARDS

ATTUNING TO A NEW DECK

If you have a new deck of tarot cards, attune to them for seven days before you read with them. Sleep with your cards under your pillow, and look at them every day so that you get to know them. Touch them to imprint your energy on them. The more connected you feel to your cards, the more accurate, insightful, and inspiring your readings can be.

SHUFFLING THE DECK

Whenever you shuffle, relax and allow your feelings and questions to surface. Take as long as you need for this.

The two most frequently used methods to select cards for a reading are as follows:
* Lay out all the cards face down in a fan shape. Then, use your left hand (the hand of fate) to choose the appropriate number of cards one by one.
* Alternatively, stack the shuffled deck face down and cut it twice so you have three piles of cards. Choose one pile to become the top of the deck and gather up the other two piles underneath it. In this case, using your natural dominant hand, take cards in order from the top of the deck.

If you are reading cards for another person, ask them to choose cards from a fan shape you have laid down, or ask them to shuffle and cut the deck. The card layouts, or "spreads," are described on pages 7 to 12.

You may feel comfortable reading the cards without the interpretations on pages 14 to 64; or you may consult the interpretations, but get other messages as you conduct your card reading.
The more you practice, the more natural it will feel to trust the impressions and messages you receive.

Protecting and Cleansing the Deck

When you are not using your cards, keep them wrapped in a natural cloth (such as cotton or silk) of a dark color (such as deep purple). Some tarot readers also use this as a "reading cloth," laying the cards on the cloth for their readings to help keep the cards clean. Store them in a box away from sunlight, perhaps protecting them with a favorite crystal—such as clear quartz (the "master" crystal) or amethyst (for healing, insight, and protection).

When you take out your cards for a reading, gently blow on them to clear away the old energy within them. Some tarot readers like to knock once on the top of the deck for the same effect.

WHAT TO DO IF YOU CAN'T MAKE SENSE OF A READING

If you are confused by the cards in your reading, the following are the best ways to gain clarity.

- Ask a friend to help you to interpret the cards.

- Shuffle and lay the cards again, this time rephrasing the question or making it more specific.

- If you want to ask exactly the same question, wait three days, then try again—now is not the right time. (In particular, if you turn over the Ten of Moths, you have too much going on to find an answer.)

PAST, PRESENT, AND FUTURE

IF YOU LEARN ONLY ONE TAROT LAYOUT, THIS SHOULD BE IT—THE CLASSIC "PAST, PRESENT, AND FUTURE." IT WORKS NO MATTER HOW SIMPLE OR COMPLEX YOUR QUERY AND PROVIDES INSIGHT ON HOW YOUR PAST MIGHT INFLUENCE YOU, HOW YOUR LIFE IS NOW, AND WHERE YOUR LIFE WILL TAKE YOU.

1 Think about your situation as you shuffle the deck (see page 6). If you are reading for someone else, ask him or her to shuffle.

2 When you are ready, either fan out the cards or cut the deck and take three cards. Lay out the cards as shown below.

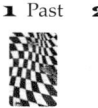

1 Past   **2** Present   **3** Future

To find out more about any of these life stages, shuffle the cards again, then choose one more card and place it face up next to the existing card in the appropriate position. For example, if you wanted to know more about the future, place a new card next to the existing future card, and interpret the two cards in light of each other.

8 LAYING THE CARDS

SPIRIT MESSAGES

THIS TWO-CARD READING IS BASED ON THE SPIRITUALIST PRACTICE OF PLACING TWO CHALKBOARDS FACE TO FACE AND BINDING THEM TOGETHER. DURING A SÉANCE, THE BOARDS WOULD BE OPENED TO REVEAL A SPIRIT MESSAGE WRITTEN IN CHALK.

1 Think about your question as you shuffle the deck. Ask the cards to send you a message to help you. When you are ready, place the deck face down on the table. Using your left hand, split the deck into two piles, placed side by side.

2 Take the top card from the left pile with your left hand and the top card from the right pile with your right hand. Carefully press the cards to each other, faces together. Place them on the table so that the left-hand card is at the bottom and the right-hand card is on the top, keeping the faces together.

3 Open out the cards as if they were the pages of a book. The card on the left is you or your situation or question, and the card on the right is the outcome. Look up the meanings on pages 14 to 64. Of course, your intuition may also give you the answers.

LAYING THE CARDS 9

ASK THREE TIMES

THIS TAROT SPREAD IS KNOWN AS "ASK THREE TIMES" AND IT WILL GIVE YOU A YES OR NO ANSWER TO A SPECIFIC QUESTION, WITHOUT THE NEED FOR LAYERS OF INTERPRETATION.

1 Shuffle the deck, then fan it out, face down (see page 6). Close your eyes and ask your question. With your left hand, choose one card from the fan and place it, still face down, in front of you.

2 Do this twice more, each time asking the same question before you pick the card. You should have three cards face down next to each other.

3 Turn over the cards and look at the list opposite to determine if they are yes, no, or neutral cards. Three yes cards gives you a certain yes answer; two yes cards (with one no or neutral card) means a positive outcome is most likely, but it may take time to come about. Three no cards, two nos and a yes, or a mixture of no and neutral cards, gives you a negative answer. Predominantly or only neutral cards is an inconclusive reading.

NEUTRAL CARDS

TWO OF BEES
FOUR OF BEES
FOUR OF DRAGONFLIES
FIVE OF MOTHS
SEVEN OF MOTHS
THE HERMIT
THE HANGED MAN

NO CARDS

THREE OF BEES
FIVE OF BEES
SIX OF BEES
SEVEN OF BEES
EIGHT OF BEES
NINE OF BEES
TEN OF BEES
KNIGHT OF BEES
TEN OF MOTHS
FIVE OF DRAGONFLIES
SEVEN OF DRAGONFLIES
EIGHT OF DRAGONFLIES
FIVE OF BEETLES
DEATH
THE DEVIL
THE TOWER
THE MOON

YES CARDS

All other cards.

10 LAYING THE CARDS

TO ANSWER A QUESTION

THE FOLLOWING TAROT SPREAD WILL GIVE YOU MORE DETAIL THAN A SIMPLE YES OR NO ANSWER. IT WILL HELP ILLUMINATE EVENTS FROM YOUR PAST OR PRESENT, AS WELL AS REVEAL HIDDEN INFLUENCES AND ATTITUDES AROUND YOU, AND ADVISE ON HOW YOU MIGHT NEGOTIATE THE PATH AHEAD.

Think of your question as you shuffle the cards. Using your left hand, choose seven cards, laying them from left to right in a horseshoe shape, as shown.

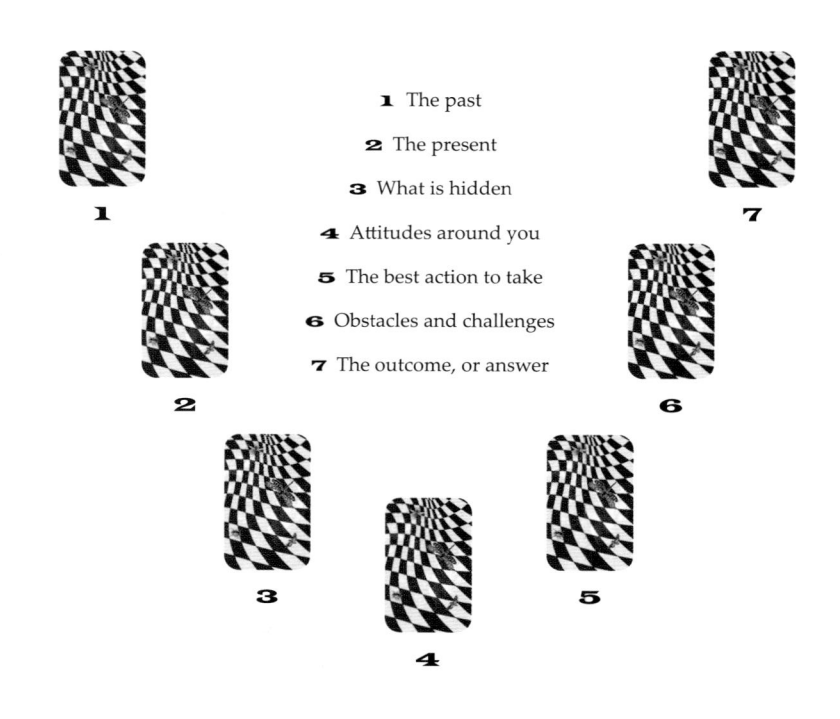

1 The past

2 The present

3 What is hidden

4 Attitudes around you

5 The best action to take

6 Obstacles and challenges

7 The outcome, or answer

LAYING THE CARDS 11

THE WEEK AHEAD AND YEAR AHEAD

TIMING SPREADS, SUCH AS THE WEEK AHEAD SPREAD AND THE YEAR AHEAD SPREAD, ARE GREAT WAYS TO GET A SENSE OF HOW A CERTAIN PERIOD OF TIME WILL UNFOLD.

For either layout, shuffle the deck and fan or cut the cards.

THE WEEK AHEAD

Choose eight cards—a Significator and one card for each day of the week. The Significator is a central, single card that expresses the underlying theme of the reading. Lay this card first. Around it in a circle, lay out the other cards as shown. The interpretation of each card in the circle will give you an insight into the events, challenges, or inspirations of the relevant day.

THE YEAR AHEAD

Choose 13 cards, beginning with a Significator (see above), which you place in the center of an imaginary clock face. Lay down one card for each month of the year, beginning at one o'clock and ending at twelve o'clock. The card at position one symbolizes the present month, the card at position two represents the next month, and so on.

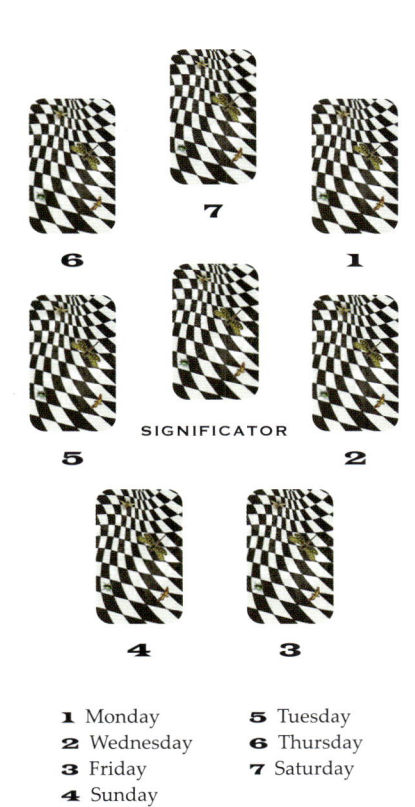

1 Monday
2 Wednesday
3 Friday
4 Sunday
5 Tuesday
6 Thursday
7 Saturday

12 LAYING THE CARDS

THE CROSS

LIKE THE PAST, PRESENT, AND FUTURE SPREAD (SEE PAGE 7), THE CROSS IS A POPULAR LAYOUT AND WELL WORTH MASTERING. THIS SPREAD TAKES A DEEPER LOOK AT THE CHALLENGES AND INFLUENCES AROUND YOU IN THE PAST, PRESENT, AND FUTURE. THE KEY CARDS ARE CARD NINE (HOPES AND FEARS) AND CARD FOUR (HIDDEN REASONS)—THESE OFTEN EXPLAIN OUR MOTIVATION AND PASSIONS. YOU CAN TRY A MINI-VERSION OF THE CROSS, USING JUST THE FIRST SIX CARDS, IF YOU PREFER.

1. You as you are now
2. What is complementing or crossing you
3. The best that can happen at present
4. The hidden reason for your situation or question
5. The past
6. What happens next
7. Your prospects
8. Your environment and how others see you
9. Hopes and fears
10. The outcome

THE CARDS AND THEIR MEANINGS

THE MAJOR ARCANA

CARDS 0 TO XXI REPRESENT THE MAJOR ARCANA OF THE TAROT. THESE 22 CARDS SHOW LIFE'S TURNING POINTS OR MAJOR ISSUES AND EVENTS. THEY HOLD THE PRIMARY ENERGIES OF THE TAROT.

INTERPRETATION AND MEANING

The major arcana sequence is a journey—worldly through to spiritual—ending with The World before returning to card 0, The Fool, a symbolic rebirth as the cycle of life continues. The Wheel of Fortune (Card X) reminds us that no matter how we seek to control events or how confidently we may assume certain outcomes, fate is at work and there are influences beyond our control. The meanings of the cards are not always transparent. For example, Death (Card XIII) does not denote physical death, but transition.

The major arcana can represent the stages of our life—the innocence of youth in The Fool, creative ambition in the Magician, and family and abundance in The Empress.

Every card has a special message, and you will find that certain cards reappear in your readings to remind you that the message is still relevant to you.

STARTING OUT

If you are a beginner, you might like to gain confidence by reading only with the cards of the major arcana at first. Once you know these cards well, you can introduce the minor arcana to bring further insight to your readings.

UNDERSTANDING REVERSALS

Traditionally, all tarot cards have both upright and reversed meanings. A reversed meaning is often negative, but in some cases can be more positive than an upright meaning. If a reversed card doesn't feel right to you, read both the upright and reversed card meanings and choose which meaning resonates most. It is also worth bearing in mind that some tarot readers do not read reversals at all; if reversed cards appear in a reading, they simply turn them the right way up, then begin the tarot reading. Choose whatever feels right for you.

THE MAJOR ARCANA

THE MESSAGE: Follow your dream and take a leap of faith.

THE FOOL

ELEMENT: **AIR**
PLANET: **URANUS**
KEY WORDS: **RISK, DREAMS, A NEW PATH**

Curious about the world, The Fool prepares to follow his dream, leaping into unknown territory. The white rose represents his innocence; his number 0 (represented by the shape of the blue egg) reminds us of his zero experience. He is about to embark upon a risky journey with little but his ideals to sustain him. The Victorian dog figurine—a spaniel—brings to mind Queen Victoria's beloved companion, Dash, here symbolizing the world of comfort and possessions that The Fool leaves behind. The mountains represent the freedom and challenges ahead. If The Fool can take this leap of faith, the magic butterfly of transformation awaits.

In your reading, it's time to start over, going your own way with renewed energy. You can travel light, leaving heavy baggage—emotional or otherwise—behind you. You have a special opportunity for adventure that could lead to fun and entertainment, something you need right now. The Fool may also represent a young person leaving home.

REVERSED: The reversed Fool leaps before he looks. Spontaneity and idealism is not the right approach for you just now. Hold back and examine the detail.

[I] THE MAGICIAN

PLANET: **MERCURY**
KEY WORDS: **ENERGY, COMMUNICATION, TRAVEL**

Like the phenomenal Victorian escapologist Harry Houdini or the conjuror Evanion, The Magician is a true showman. With him are his assistants Dragonfly, Moth, Bee, and Beetle, the symbols of the four tarot suits that represent the four elements of our world—Water, Fire, Air, and Earth. Waving his magic wand, The Magician draws upon these infinite resources to create whatever he chooses. Like the Strength card (Card VIII), he has the magical symbol known as the lemniscate, or figure-eight, which represents infinity and focus.

In your reading, The Magician shows creativity, action, and positive change. You will make practical decisions, while your lateral thinking will help you solve problems so that you can make progress in your life. What you desire can manifest.

This is a time for important journeys and, along with the Flying Machine (Card VII), and the Three and Eight of Moths in the minor arcana, the Magician with his hot-air balloon predicts travel and broadening horizons. All offers are worth exploring.

REVERSED: In reverse, The Magician represents trickery. A person or situation that looks appealing may deceive you. There may be a delay to your travel plans or projects you have in development. Look carefully at others' motives and double-check arrangements.

THE MESSAGE: Express your ideas and take action.

THE MAJOR ARCANA

The Message: Let your intuition guide you.

NOTE: Comment on Daniel Dunglas Home from *The First Psychic: The Peculiar Mystery of a Notorious Victorian Wizard*, Peter Lamont (Abacus, 2006).

II THE HIGH PRIESTESS

PLANET: **THE MOON**

KEY WORDS: **SECRETS, LEARNING, PSYCHIC DEVELOPMENT**

From the mid-1800s it was not unusual to partake of a spiritualist séance, where invited guests sat in a circle for spirit communion. One of the most celebrated mediums of this time was the Scot Daniel Dunglas Home, who channeled spirits and seemed to disappear from one room and reappear in another. Like him, The High Priestess walks between two worlds – the Earth plane and the Spirit realm.

The crystal ball tells us that this is the card of clairvoyance, while the sacred book denotes knowledge. The pomegranate fruit represents creativity, and the Moon symbolizes the feminine principle, the psyche, dreams, and otherworldly wisdom, and also echoes the Moon-Crown of Isis, Queen of Egyptian magic. The High Priestess's face is enclosed in a locket, representing privacy and enclosure.

In your reading, the High Priestess asks you to rely on your intuition rather than facts. You may discover secrets. She may also represent education, a good mentor, and spiritual development—you might soon connect with a spirit guide. Pay attention to your dreams and other messages from your sixth sense. Trust your knowing.

REVERSED: There is unnecessary secrecy in situations that should engender open communication. You may be under the influence of poor guidance or trusting in the wrong person. Perhaps you are following a path that is not right for you.

THE MAJOR ARCANA 17

☐ III THE EMPRESS

PLANET: **VENUS**

KEY WORDS: **ABUNDANCE, FERTILITY, THE MOTHER, LOVE, HARMONY**

The Empress is Queen Victoria, Empress of India. She is the consort of Card IV, The Emperor, represented by Prince Albert. As mother to nine children, Queen Victoria provides the perfect mother archetype. The corn meadow reflects her fertility; the apple tree, an emblem of the generations, symbolizes relationships, children, and family. Pink roses and a cherub denote love, affection, and the nurturing qualities of the matriarch. She is the embodiment of feminine qualities.

In your reading, The Empress is a sign that your emotional and financial needs will be met, and that you are entering a time of great productivity and happiness. The Empress offers comfort without materialism and love without conditions. She can also herald a pregnancy, or the positive influence of a mother or mother-figure in your life. She indicates a time when family life thrives and great creativity and productivity pervade all your projects.

REVERSED: You may encounter household problems, or a lack of love and support because of the absence of a mother-figure or her nurturing qualities in your life. The reversed Empress may also indicate financial problems.

THE MESSAGE: Love what you do.

THE MAJOR ARCANA

Message: Practical help and organization.

IV THE EMPEROR

ZODIAC SIGN: **ARIES**
KEY WORDS: **DOMINION, STRENGTH, LOGIC, ORGANIZATION, ADVICE**

The Emperor is Prince Albert. He is the father archetype, a protector, and leader who represents logic, action, and strategy. He is the counterbalance to his consort, The Empress, who illustrates conventional feminine qualities. The heraldic eagle was the insignia of Roman emperors and shows his high status, while the astrological glyph denotes the sign of Aries, showing that he has both authority and determination. The domed building is London's Crystal Palace, designed by Sir Joseph Paxton for the Great Exhibition of 1851, a showcase for world innovation in industry and the arts that was devised by Prince Albert himself.

In your reading, The Emperor brings solutions and can represent an authoritative man who can provide help and advice. He may sometimes be domineering and stubborn, but you can rely on him. If you are facing a difficult decision, he will be a good ally, just take care to look closely at the details and don't be swayed by a forceful personality. If your question is about love, The Emperor shows a future partner or husband.

Reversed: You may feel oppressed and bullied. The reversed Emperor denotes an individual who does not use his power wisely and puts unreasonable pressure on others. With regard to a certain situation, the reversed Emperor warns us that traditional attitudes cause upset.

ⅴ THE HIGH PRIEST

ZODIAC SIGN: **TAURUS**
KEY WORDS: **AUTHORITY, UNITY, EDUCATION**

The Hierophant is The High Priest, twinned with The High Priestess. Both mediate between Heaven and Earth, but the Hierophant works in public rather than in private. He is traditionally seen as a priest or the Pope, wearing a triple crown. His symbol is the crossed keys, which represent Saint Peter's keys to the gates of Heaven and are an emblem of his spiritual authority.

In your reading, The Hierophant tells you that education and learning are the way to spiritual and earthly advancement. He represents a positive mentor in your life, such as a teacher. The Hierophant can predict a wedding, and he also expresses the principle of unity through marriage. Symbolically, he represents the unification of body, mind, and spirit, or of ideals and practice. He heralds wisdom, authority, support, and self-acceptance.

REVERSED: You may experience a lack of unity, particularly in situations that involve groups of people, such as in the workplace or at school. There may be leadership issues, divisions, and factions. As a result, the reversed Hierophant represents mistrust.

THE MESSAGE: Take counsel.

THE MAJOR ARCANA

VI THE LOVERS

ZODIAC SIGN: **GEMINI**
KEY WORDS: **LOVE, SELF-COMPASSION, CHOICES**

Cupid, his fan held high, reveals himself as the messenger of love. In several nineteenth-century tarots, there are three people in The Lovers card (indicating a love triangle); in others, The Lovers are the biblical Adam and Eve. Here, we have a clockwork heart, to indicate that it is not only time for love, but that an imminent decision will be made.

In your reading, The Lovers promises you that love is coming. It is also a reminder that love means maturity and choosing the right partner or path. You should look to long-term happiness rather than trying to fulfill only short-term desires. The Lovers asks you also how much you love yourself. Look at familiar patterns in your life and establish whether or not they still serve you. If not, perhaps it's time to make a choice that leads you more firmly toward future happiness. There would be much to gain.

REVERSED: In reverse, this card represents an unhappy relationship, or separation from a partner. You may be on the verge of a poor decision—the card is a warning that you need to take time to consider your options more carefully. The reversed Lovers may also indicate that you're taking an easy way out, rather than facing a challenge head-on.

THE MESSAGE: Love is coming, and a decision.

ⅦTHE FLYING MACHINE

ZODIAC SIGN: **CANCER**
KEY WORDS: **PROGRESS, DETERMINATION, TRAVEL**

The Flying Machine echoes the wonderful aerial inventions of the Victorian era, when Count Ferdinand von Zeppelin invented the airship and the Wright Brothers their record-breaking biplane. This was the era of amazing, steam-powered contraptions built at great speed in an attempt to win the race to put men (and later women) in the air. Here, two chess pieces are used to construct a mechanical flying machine. They symbolize the light and dark aspects of our desires. To make progress we must be in control of our own machine—the inner workings of our minds and bodies.

The Flying Machine shows willpower, speed, goal setting, and determination. Progress and victory are certain. In the past you may have experienced pressure and struggled to steer your course. Perhaps you had to manage difficult people and projects. This card shows that you will succeed through sheer force of personality and dedication. The Flying Machine can also represent an important journey and, on a lighter note, a new vehicle. No matter how it manifests, this card tells you that you are moving on.

REVERSED: Ego and intense emotions rule as you or someone close gets a situation out of perspective, halting progress toward a goal. Travel plans may be delayed.

THE MESSAGE: Speed, a major departure.

22 THE MAJOR ARCANA

THE MESSAGE: A compassionate response to challenges.

VIII STRENGTH

ZODIAC SIGN: **LEO**
KEY WORDS: **STRENGTH, HEALTH, PATIENCE**

Along with Justice (Card XI) and Temperance (Card XIV), Strength is one of the virtue cards in the tarot. It represents tension between our base instinct (the lion) and our higher selves (the rose). Although the lion's head is mounted on a plaque, his wildness tamed, he can still strike fear into those who look upon him. Like The Magician (Card I), Strength is shown with the lemniscate or figure-eight symbol, representing infinity and, in this case, strength of purpose.

In your reading, Strength heralds health, patience, and moral fortitude. It indicates a desire for peace and to protect others, and a commitment to others and projects. It reminds you that, faced with a difficult opponent, confrontation and force are not the answer—it is much better to show compassion and grace. You can succeed if you are patient. If you have a question about health, Strength reveals recovery and energy.

REVERSED: In reverse, Strength represents fear, hesitancy, and avoidable danger, and is a sign that your energy levels may be low. Think of moving forward in small steps, rather than feeling overwhelmed by all you have to do.

IX THE HERMIT

ZODIAC SIGN: **VIRGO**
KEY WORDS: **SOLITUDE, ANALYSIS, TIME**

The Hermit steps aside from society to spend time alone to find his truth. He is often depicted with a lantern to guide him on his path, and we also see an hourglass, as The Hermit was once known as Father Time. He also carries a staff topped with an aquamarine crystal, which represents courage, peace, and protection. A mechanical snake entwines itself around the staff and symbolizes Asclepius, the Greek god of healing. The butterflies in the webs indicate time spent away from everyday activities.

In your reading, the Hermit signals that there will be time for you to feed your soul—through education, reading, or travel—or even to go on a pilgrimage. You will temporarily leave your everyday concerns to help you heal or develop spiritually. A period of solitude will be your active choice so you can process your thoughts and emotions. This is not an exile, but a positive time in which you can nurture yourself. This is a card of analysis and suggests that you need, or will have, time to fully consider a situation.

REVERSED: In reverse, this card represents enforced isolation at a time when you would prefer support from others. However, it can also denote that your sense of isolation stems from your own fear of rejection, rather than the reality of a situation.

THE MESSAGE: A time for retreat and healing.

24 THE MAJOR ARCANA

THE MESSAGE: Good luck comes your way.

⊠ THE WHEEL OF FORTUNE

PLANET: **JUPITER**
KEY WORDS: **FATE, LUCK, CHANGE**

As the tenth card in the tarot, The Wheel of Fortune is the cycle's halfway point and denotes a sudden change. It is a symbol of fate—above the wheel there is blue sky and below is the storm of misfortune. The four suit symbols of moth, bee, dragonfly, and beetle are linked to the four elements and show that anything is possible when the wheel turns.

In your reading, The Wheel of Fortune reveals a turn for the better. You can expect improvements in your life—including in your finances. Your openness and energy help attract new people to you and provide you with choices. There are new horizons to explore and now is the time to say yes to whatever opportunities come your way. Make the most of these gifts while they last.

You may interpret The Wheel as a psychic card because of its associations with fate and destiny. If you have a question about your spiritual development, this card shows you are on the right path.

REVERSED: You may experience a downturn in your fortunes, but the change is entirely out of your hands. Make the experience as positive as you can—there is no blame, only opportunity for growth.

XI | JUSTICE

ZODIAC SIGN: **LIBRA**
KEY WORDS: **DECISIONS, FAIRNESS, BALANCE**

This card possesses the sword of liberty and the scales of justice. Justice is one of the tarot's virtue cards—along with Strength (Card VIII) and Temperance (Card XIV). Representing fairness, Justice shows that the law, represented by the library of books, will be upheld. She embodies the importance of evaluation, showing that this is a time for righting wrongs and redressing imbalances of any kind. The card reminds us of the importance of making considered decisions.

In your reading, if you are waiting for the outcome of a legal situation, the appearance of Justice shows that the judgment will go in your favor. You will clear any issue from your past that has held you back and you will forge ahead. This card can also predict that you will successfully complete a project. This is not a time for rash judgments—keep a level head.

REVERSED: In reverse, this card can represent a miscarriage of justice—perhaps in a literal sense in a court of law, but also in any other aspect of your life. Gather strong advocates around you and get the support you need.

THE MESSAGE: Justice is done.

XII THE HANGED MAN

PLANET: **NEPTUNE**
ELEMENT: **WATER**
KEY WORDS: **WAITING, INSIGHT, SACRIFICE**

A pendulum with a human face is suspended within an ash tree. Despite the card's name, the scene is calm, even content. The butterflies echo this suspension: they are caught in spider webs and yet come to no harm. The rune stones connect the card to the legend of the Norse god Odin, who hung from the great World Ash for nine days and nights after which he gained the gifts of prophecy and rune-reading.

In your reading, The Hanged Man shows that you may need to make a sacrifice to get something you want. This could mean that, for now, you need to let go of a dream and resolve to follow on a more realistic path. The card signifies that you're waiting for action—literally, hanging around. The Hanged Man is a sign you are in limbo. However, he also serves to remind you that you have an opportunity to change your perspective on a situation and to look at things another way.

REVERSED: There is procrastination in your life—perhaps an arrangement or a relationship has got stuck. Rather than hang on, release yourself from any unsatisfactory agreements straightaway.

THE MESSAGE: A time to wait and reconsider.

XIII DEATH

ZODIAC SIGN: **SCORPIO**
KEY WORDS: **TRANSITION, ENDINGS, BEGINNINGS**

The Victorians experienced high rates of mortality, so they embraced death as part of life and ritualized their mourning. On this card the X-ray (a machine invented during Victorian times) reveals the skeleton of a hand. Next to this is a human skull. Rather than symbolizing death itself, these emblems remind us that death leaves us with the basics, the bare bones of our existence.

The solitary raven at sunset depicts that death is a state of transition. In the Irish epic tale Táin Bó Cúailnge, the dark goddess Morrigan shape-shifts into a raven to give strange prophecies. She lands on the shoulder of the hero Cú Chulainn, symbolizing his imminent death. The cameo locket depicts an open rose and rosebud—reminding us that as one aspect of ourselves ends, we make way for regeneration.

Death does not mean physical death, but the end of an era. For you to progress you need to let go of that which you no longer need. That might be an unfulfilling career or relationship, an unhappy home, or outdated attitudes. The Death card leaves us with the basics—the bare bones of our existence. Letting go can be tough, but it clears the way ahead for a period of renewal and reinvention.

REVERSED: In reverse, this card reminds you that change will happen even if you resist it. Perhaps you feel something is being unfairly taken from you. There is no other option for now; accept what is.

THE MESSAGE: Let go and look forward.

THE MAJOR ARCANA

THE MESSAGE: Time for reconciliation.

XIV TEMPERANCE

ZODIAC SIGN: **SAGITTARIUS**
KEY WORDS: **BALANCE, RECONCILIATION, ALCHEMY**

One of the tarot's virtue cards, along with Strength (Card VIII) and Justice (Card XI), Temperance takes the form of an angel. Traditionally, the angel is Archangel Michael, the angel of protection. No drop of water is spilled from the goblets, which symbolize the need for precision, balance, and perhaps a miracle or two. The flowers are irises, named after the Greek goddess of hope. The dragonfly's element is water, symbolizing emotion.

In your reading, Temperance shows that there may be many things you need to manage in your life. Getting your life to work feels like a fine balancing act just now. Persistent effort, the ability to adapt, and attention to detail will get you through.

This card also predicts reconciliation between people. It provides a hopeful sign that you will be able to heal rifts and restore harmony in certain relationships.

REVERSED: Demands upon you may feel overwhelming, causing you emotional upset. Difficult issues from the past could surface and you may experience a lack of money or other resources. Slow down, and go one step at a time.

XV THE DEVIL

ZODIAC SIGN: **CAPRICORN**
KEY WORDS: **ADDICTION, HABIT, SELF-RESTRICTION**

The Devil could represent Satan—the fallen angel and a symbol of evil and temptation; or it may denote the God Pan, the Roman god of excess. In tarot, the two chained birds and creeping ivy (the Victorians' favored graveside gift) remind us that The Devil embodies addiction or enslavement. This may apply equally to affairs, unhealthy relationships, and ill-advised contracts, as well as to substances.

In your reading, The Devil shows you your conflicted self—it is fear or guilt that keeps you trapped, rather than any actual "deal with the devil." You are tied to a person or situation out of habit; you may be locked in a pattern of avoidance. The appearance of The Devil reminds you that, in reality, you can choose to be free of his influence at any point. It is time to recognize your rightful needs and to walk away from anything or anyone who demands your loyalty, but offers little of real or long-lasting value in return.

REVERSED: In reverse, this card symbolizes manipulation that you can resist, no matter how forceful it feels. The ties that bind are just an illusion.

THE MESSAGE: You can choose to be free.

THE MAJOR ARCANA

THE MESSAGE: Rebuild from the ruins.

XVI | THE TOWER

PLANET: **MARS**
KEY WORDS: **DESTRUCTION, RELEASE**

Destroyed by lightning and fire, The Tower is also known as La Maison de Dieu, or House of God. Just as God struck down the tower of Babel in the book of Genesis, lightning strikes The Tower of the tarot. The two porcelain Victorian dolls falling helplessly into the flames show our human fragility. In Tibetan tradition, however, the sacred devotional object, the djore, or thunderbolt, represents purification of the mind in order to eliminate negative karma.

In your reading, The Tower shows that an aspect of your life may suddenly end—a relationship, a job, or a way of living. This may be shocking and painful, but you now have an opportunity to examine your life and create a new structure. On a positive note, when The Tower collapses, you let go of the stress that has been holding things together. This release of negative energy leads to a shift in consciousness, and a letting go of ego.

REVERSED: You could have avoided a situation of repression and disaster. Did you build your beliefs on assumptions? Whatever the situation, don't suffer further by blaming yourself.

XVII THE STAR

ZODIAC SIGN: **AQUARIUS**
KEY WORDS: **GUIDANCE, INSPIRATION, CREATIVITY**

The Star card shows eight stars with eight points. Eight is the number of renewal, and symbolizes a time to invent and reinvent yourself. Your guiding star dominates the sky, showing the way ahead and offering hope and inspiration. The waters of the conscious and unconscious self flow together as an angel looks to the heavenly stars, revealing that it is time to live in the light.

In your reading, The Star illuminates your path in life, reassuring you that you will be guided to your next life-stage. If you have a creative enterprise, now is the time to follow that dream. You have the resources you need to make it happen—ideas, memories, experience, originality, and energy. The Star is also a wonderful affirmation for a new career or relationship, which will thrive.

REVERSED: It may not be possible to make your dreams a reality just now. Perhaps you have a creative block, or the timing simply isn't right. Stay grounded and reassess the situation in practical terms. Beware of anyone with fantastical offers.

THE MESSAGE: Express yourself. You are guided.

THE MAJOR ARCANA

THE MESSAGE: An emotional decision.

NOTE: John Dillwyn Llewelyn (1810–1882), a photographic pioneer, along with his daughter, Thereza, took the first pictures of the surface of the moon from 1857 from his observatory in Swansea, South Wales.

XVIII THE MOON

ZODIAC SIGN: **PISCES**
KEY WORDS: **CRISIS, ILLUSION, CHOICES**

With its howling hound and wolf, water, and flying fish, The Moon represents an uncomfortable choice. The fish is a sign of the soul and of the true self. It yearns for adventure and fulfillment, but is torn between swimming in familiar waters and leaping into the new, strange terrain beyond the towers. The shimmering moon symbolizes the subconscious and is a place of magic in ancient tales. The Victorian pioneer John Dillwyn Llewelyn only increased our passion for the white planet when he took the first ever photographs of the moon's surface in 1857.

In your reading, The Moon heralds a crisis of faith or a period of emotional turmoil. You will need to make a decision, but the facts are not yet clear and what you see may be illusion. Step back, because if you look objectively into the darkness, you will glimpse the way ahead.

Although old fears may resurface, The Moon represents a time of creativity when imagination, romance, and intuition rule. Pay attention to your dreams as they hold messages for you.

REVERSED: In reverse, this card represents disillusion and being misled. There may also be an element of avoidance. You have an opportunity to make a profound and beneficial change in your affairs, but you risk letting this opportunity pass you by.

XIX THE SUN

PLANET: **THE SUN**
KEY WORDS: **GROWTH, HAPPINESS, HEALTH**

The Sun is a paradise where nature flourishes. Once the most loved motif of Victorian esthetes, who believed in the ideal of art for itself, the sunflowers symbolize purity and growth. The Victorian box hedge sets safe boundaries and provides protection from the powerful rays of the sun. The twin cherubs denote children and happiness, and symbolize the aspects of the self in harmony.

In your reading, The Sun brings good news. A new, sunny chapter is about to begin, bringing you success and acknowledgment. There may be news about a child, or you may wish to return to the carefree innocence of your childhood—perhaps with a vacation away from home or through a period of rest. If you have a project to nurture, The Sun reveals that you will feel inspired to make it happen. This is a time to flourish.

REVERSED: You deserve a break, but there seem to be obstacles in your path. However, take heart—The Sun is a positive card, even when reversed, and any setbacks will not detain you for long.

THE MESSAGE: The light of joy and success shines upon you.

THE MAJOR ARCANA

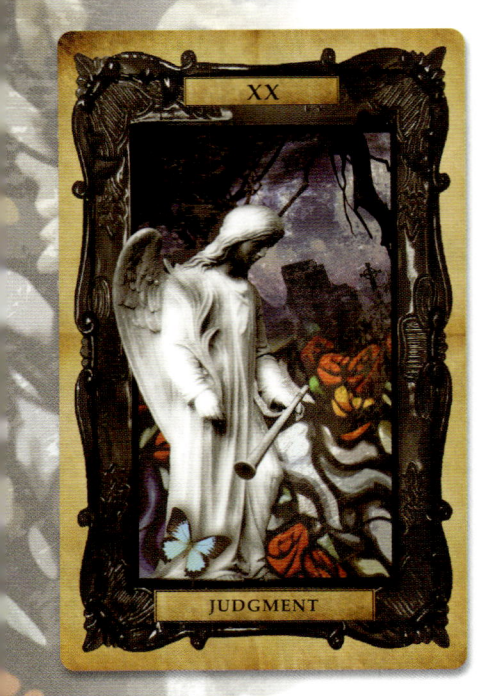

THE MESSAGE: Rise again.

XX JUDGMENT

ELEMENT: **FIRE**
PLANET: **PLUTO**
KEY WORDS: **JUDGMENT, THE PAST, SECOND CHANCES**

How do we judge ourselves? A Victorian mortuary angel sounds a trumpet, a wake-up call. The angel, watching over our soul, asks us to assess our past actions before we close a certain chapter (symbolized by the distant graveyard) in our lives. The blue butterfly reminds us of the butterflies in the first card—The Fool (0)—because we are approaching the end of one tarot cycle and we will begin our spiritual journey all over again.

In your reading, The Judgment card calls time on a situation or life phase. Look back over the course of that phase, revisit it in your mind, then lay it to rest. Thankfully, this reminiscence is a rewarding process, one that is filled with a sense of pleasure rather than with regret. The card's alternative title is Fame, so now may be an opportunity to blow your own trumpet and acknowledge your successes.

The Judgment card also represents a second chance. You have a window of opportunity to right any wrongs, or to try again in a relationship or a job, for example. The wake-up call can also be spiritual—it may be a call to divine service.

REVERSED: In reverse, the Judgment card represents slowed progress and delayed plans. You may be unable to let go of the past—don't dwell on unresolved problems, move forward.

XXI THE WORLD

PLANET: **SATURN**
KEY WORDS: **REWARD, COMPLETION, SUCCESS**

A card of joy and completion, The World represents wholeness. As the last card of the major arcana, The World denotes happy endings. The celestial cherubs hold the world aloft as an example of serene perfection, a situation where Heaven and Earth meet in absolute harmony.

In your reading, The World shows you that parts of your self or your life have come together in harmony. It heralds the successful completion of a particular phase in your life, along with rewards and celebrations—perhaps for an anniversary or a graduation. Representing agreement, The World predicts the end of conflict and tension. You may have opportunities to travel, and you may experience a great achievement in your career, happiness in your relationship, and further spiritual development. Like the unified cosmos, you can experience spiritual oneness with the world.

REVERSED: You have a need to stay safe rather than move on to greater things. Outdated attitudes or values keep you stuck in one place. It is time to put an end to procrastination and to look further afield for inspiration.

THE MESSAGE: Appreciate success and enjoy life.

THE MINOR ARCANA

THE FOUR SUITS OF THE MINOR ARCANA—TRADITIONALLY, CUPS, WANDS, SWORDS, AND PENTACLES OR COINS—ARE THOUGHT TO HAVE DERIVED FROM THE PLAYING CARDS OR ELEVENTH-CENTURY CHINA AND KOREA.

INTERPRETATION AND MEANINGS

While the cards of the major arcana (see pages 13–35) show significant, lasting influences and themes in our lives, the cards of the minor arcana express day-to-day events. The cards in each suit are numbered from Ace to Ten and also include four court cards—Page, Knight, Queen, and King. Each suit is associated with an element, which expresses that suit's qualities:

THE ELEMENT OF WATER (DRAGONFLIES): emotions; "I feel."

THE ELEMENT OF FIRE (MOTHS): actions, intuition; "I do" or "I desire."

THE ELEMENT OF AIR (BEES): thoughts; "I think."

THE ELEMENT OF EARTH (BEETLES): objects, sensation; "I possess."

NUMBER MEANINGS

The meanings attributed to each card number vary according to the suit in question. Although the individual card meanings are specific, the general number meanings take us on a journey, and the stages (themes) of that journey offer a perspective that may be applied to all the suits:

ACES: Beginnings
TWOS: Partnership, balance
THREES: Creation
FOURS: Stability
FIVES: Challenges
SIXES: Harmony
SEVENS: Potential
EIGHTS: Change
NINES: Expression
TENS: Excess, release

COURT CARD MEANINGS

The Page, Knight, Queen, and King in each suit suggest an individual or a general influence. The descriptions over the following pages give both interpretations so that you can choose whichever feels right in your reading. Always go with your feelings rather than become distracted by analyzing why.

THE MINOR ARCANA 37

THE SUIT OF DRAGONFLIES

THE ELEMENT OF WATER

TRADITIONAL TAROT SUIT OF CUPS

ACE OF DRAGONFLIES

This Ace brings the gifts of love and creation, which may come to you as a new relationship or project, a pregnancy, or another aspect of motherhood. The element of this suit is Water, which represents the emotions; whatever you do from the heart is favored now. You may show love and affection and nurture it in others. The Dragonfly holds a moonstone, a symbol of femininity, intuition, and empathy.

REVERSED: You may experience difficulties in relationships and possibly conception—in terms of fertility issues, delayed projects and blocks to self-expression. There could be an outpouring of negative or overwhelming emotion just now.

TWO OF DRAGONFLIES

Partnership. This card indicates a relationship that forms out of love, affection, and respect. The Two predicts romance and meeting the partner you need. You are ready to share and find a soul mate. This card can also represent strong friendships, and sensitivity in your dealings with others.

REVERSED: A partnership is out of balance and emotions run high. This influence will pass, so it is best to hold back on making major decisions about relationships until you reach calmer waters and know who—and what—you are dealing with.

THREE OF DRAGONFLIES

The Three indicates a happy time of high spirits, celebration, and laughter. Whatever your recent circumstances, friends and family gather round as parties and other outings beckon. This card also represents pregnancies and naming ceremonies, such as Christenings. You enjoy others' company and appreciate relationships both old and new.

REVERSED: The reversed card shows excess and indulgence, disappointment in others' actions and attitudes, and also distance between people. There may also be infidelity or another betrayal, which may be subtle. Stress may cause or contribute to health problems.

FOUR OF DRAGONFLIES

Although this card shows stability, you may be stuck in old patterns of behavior, beginning to feel bored and static. While this may be acceptable in the short term, if you are complacent, a relationship or project may deteriorate. Take action before you lose motivation.

REVERSED: Dissatisfaction, restlessness, and boredom are becoming more evident. A situation has been allowed to continue for too long, so you may now be feeling trapped. Make a decision and be free.

FIVE OF DRAGONFLIES

With its emphasis on sorrow and loss, the Five often shows a time of regret and upset. Emotions run high and hidden problems come out into the open. This is a time to take an honest look at a relationship, project, or career path that is not working out and plan how you might salvage what is left. Heal the wounds and move on.

REVERSED: The reversed meaning for this card is more positive than the upright meaning. It shows that you have been moving through a time of emotional upset, but that you have experienced the worst. Now you are able to move on up, putting the past firmly behind you.

SIX OF DRAGONFLIES

Nostalgia and affection enter your world as the past influences the future. Old friends may resurface, bringing with them kindness, empathy, and fond memories. You may make a discovery about some aspect of your family history or rekindle a pastime you once loved. This card can also announce a visitor.

REVERSED: News or a visit stirs up unwelcome memories. This is a time of struggle with the past and may bring relationship difficulties. Try not to dwell on what cannot be changed and instead look at how you can make positive inroads in the future.

SEVEN OF DRAGONFLIES

This is a time of great potential. Anything is possible—although ideas and opportunities are vague, so you cannot see which options are truly viable and which are fantasy. There is a sense of anticipation now as you reach a turning point, but you will need more detail before a decision can be made.

REVERSED: Disillusion. This may be an upsetting time that forces you to dramatically revise your expectations. There may be deception in a relationship, a friendship, or an offer that's made to you. What you hoped for seems unfounded; it's time to start over.

EIGHT OF DRAGONFLIES

It's time to go, but this departure comes only after due consideration. A situation or a relationship has run its course—you have given it every chance and, with sorrow, you need to free yourself from the commitment. This card can also indicate the start of a great journey.

REVERSED: You may be leaving a situation without proper consideration. Think carefully before making the leap—you could find value here that you have yet to appreciate. Alternatively, the reversed Eight can show that another's poor judgment leaves you feeling abandoned.

NINE OF DRAGONFLIES

Known as the "wish" card of the tarot, the Nine of Dragonflies is a sign that now is the time to attract whatever you wish for into your life—including a new partner and new friends. Manifest your dreams through your positive wishes and affirmations. As everything in your life improves with this Nine, this is a card of true happiness.

Reversed: This is the card of me, me, me. You may be guilty of emotional disconnection, possessiveness, vanity, and tactlessness; or, conversely, you may be treated insensitively as a result of others' self-obsession and ego. Others may not reciprocate your emotional honesty, but don't lose heart.

TEN OF DRAGONFLIES

The Ten brings continuing peace, abundance, and happiness. This is a wonderful card for family and groups, indicating contentment in relationships and between generations. The card can also predict love and family, the company of children and younger people, and family gatherings. Relationships are very rewarding.

Reversed: This is still generally a card of good fortune, although communication problems may surface. Think carefully about what you say and write to avoid misunderstandings. A love hope may be misplaced.

PAGE OF DRAGONFLIES

Young at heart and full of high spirits, the Page not only represents a sociable person, but more generally a message to have fun and feel young again. The Page is artistic, so this is a good time for creative expression. He brings with him good news about children and projects.

REVERSED: The reversed Page represents a superficial influence. Immaturity and problems with self-expression lead to frustration for those around this character. In relationship terms, the reversed Page can show a lack of commitment.

KNIGHT OF DRAGONFLIES

A promising situation. The Knight reveals a good suitor with love potential. He brings friendship and affection. However, he is a romantic dreamer, not a natural action man and, while he offers emotional support, what you see and what you get may be two different things. Observe the situation carefully.

REVERSED: Promises are broken. An individual who is full of romantic notions and gestures, the reversed Knight does not stay around long enough to see them through. For this reason, he cannot be trusted.

QUEEN OF DRAGONFLIES

A natural carer, the Queen of Dragonflies is an aspect of Card III, the Empress. Generous and popular, she is highly sensitive, artistic, and empathic, so her influence brings abundance, kindness, and love, which is represented by the roses on this card. A woman with all these characteristics may help you in all you do.

REVERSED: You may be suffering a lack of love or of resources, perhaps due to a controlling person who has withdrawn his or her affection. Try to avoid becoming caught up in the turmoil that comes with this card; this is not a situation of your making.

KING OF DRAGONFLIES

The King of Dragonflies is an aspect of Card IV, the Emperor. In a woman's reading his association with the husband archetype denotes that a big relationship is on the cards or help from a compassionate, generous individual. This King is a lover of the arts and is intuitive and sociable, so in a reading he heralds creative success. This is a good time for beginning new projects.

REVERSED: The reversed King brings with him jealousy and meanness. Turning away from love, he indicates that an individual in your life may disappoint you. This card can also mean ignoring intuition and suppressing feelings, which lead to unhappiness.

THE SUIT OF MOTHS

THE ELEMENT OF FIRE

TRADITIONAL TAROT SUIT OF WANDS

ACE OF MOTHS

This Ace brings the gifts of happiness and creativity: fertility, beginnings, ideas, energy, and invention. This is an auspicious card for a new project, business, or baby. The Moth's fiery energy, captured in the fire opal the Ace holds, brings you speed and inspiration. Communication is clear; you are perfectly connected

.
REVERSED: In relationships, the reversed Ace may show commitment issues. It may also signify fertility problems—literally and in terms of seeding new ideas or getting support for creative projects. Check travel arrangements carefully.

TWO OF MOTHS

It's time to make plans. You are moving forward now. This is a positive time, too, for finances and property, as your past work is rewarded and you can enjoy the security this brings. Connect with like-minded souls, as creative and romantic partnerships are favored. What you establish now will help your future success.

REVERSED: The reversed Two can show communication blocks, and two people may part company. There may be inequality, with only one of you committed to a future partnership or project. Save your talent for other adventures.

THREE OF MOTHS

Travel, expansion, and lots of activity are the gifts of the Three. You broaden your horizons, exploring new realms both spiritually and physically. Enjoy good fortune and new partnerships, along with myriad opportunities: an inspiring educational course, artistic projects and collaborations, or short trips away that bring you inspiration.

REVERSED: When reversed, the Three can show creative blocks and difficulties with self-expression and articulating ideas. Although travel plans may be delayed and career opportunities put on hold just now, the overall outlook is still positive.

FOUR OF MOTHS

This is the card of growth and good times, when your worries are behind you and you enjoy deserved space and freedom. It is also the card of a happy or new home, a property abroad, and honeymoons—along with special times spent with friends and loved ones, bringing both joy and contentment.

REVERSED: Narrow-mindedness curbs your need to move on. You may be restricting yourself or suffering due to others' lack of imagination. This card can also show issues with property, and particularly second homes, but any negative is temporary; the future is still bright.

FIVE OF MOTHS

There are so many strong opinions around you now that you can barely hear your own thoughts. This is a time when you are tested, and there may be potential conflict—but as long as you stand your ground and check facts and paperwork, you will succeed. In families, younger children and teens may test their parents' patience.

REVERSED: An unreliable source and even dishonesty are the messages of the reversed card. Alternatively, a negotiation turns sour and you withdraw. You feel you lose out in the process—but those who shout loudest don't always have sound advice to share.

SIX OF MOTHS

This Six is a victory card, when you triumph over past obstacles. It often predicts exam or legal success, completed projects, job interviews, promotions, and new contracts. This is a public victory, and others appreciate and applaud your achievements. You deserve every accolade; your instincts were right.

REVERSED: You may feel frustration as you wait for a positive outcome. However, this pause can be an opportunity for reflection, to look for alternative options, and to learn valuable lessons about yourself and your situation. You can still succeed.

THE MINOR ARCANA 47

SEVEN OF MOTHS

Now is the time for potential success—you have the talent and tools to do well, but it means more hard, consistent effort. You face challenges, and any success and rewards you reap will be hard won. Embrace the experience with grit and courage—be determined and focused, and reward will come.

Reversed: In the reversed position, the effort has become too much and you may be tempted to give up, even though you have the ability and are capable of doing more. Talk through your concerns and let go of self-doubt.

EIGHT OF MOTHS

The Eight is a card of travel, communication, and great news, so fly wherever your heart takes you. Journeys, action, and a happy, busy phase lie ahead with speed as your theme. At work, you may need to think on your feet when deluged by phone calls, emails, and meetings.

Reversed: Travel is delayed and/or a project is put on hold as confusion rules. It may be difficult to connect with people, particularly in business. Pay close attention to all your communications to avoid any misunderstandings. Avoid signing agreements just now.

NINE OF MOTHS

This an exciting but very demanding time, so you will need to be creative with your scheduling and tough, both emotionally and physically. You are in a strong position to build on and protect your assets as long as you look after your most precious resource—your energy. Stand firm and have patience.

REVERSED: In reverse, there is no challenge, only pressure. You will need to get through a harsh workload to keep other people happy. However, you may also resist change as a result of stubbornness. Set new, reasonable boundaries.

TEN OF MOTHS

This card represents a burden. It shows that you have far too much to do or think about and cannot see your way ahead. Drop some of your projects and responsibilities and focus on one or two things in turn to make progress. If this is one of the first cards you lay down in a reading, it's a sign that this is not a good time to read your cards—there is simply too much going on. Wait a day or two and try again.

REVERSED: Part of you needs to be incredibly busy, and you may be using work as a distraction. Conversely, others may be expecting far too much of you—this can be the card of the unreasonable boss or overly demanding family.

PAGE OF MOTHS

Messages and news arrive. Do review your arrangements and paperwork as there will be lots to organize just now. The Page of Moths connects you with others and represents a person who is eager, talkative, and full of ideas. His influence is generally positive, although you may need to double-check what he says as he tends to exaggerate.

REVERSED: Disappointing news. The reversed Page may represent a complainer in your life—he may be negative about other people to the point of manipulation and gossip. This card may also indicate problems with literacy.

KNIGHT OF MOTHS

Get ready for a surge of energy and ideas. When the Knight of Moths appears, everything speeds up, and you will not have to wait much longer to reach your goals. As a potential partner, this Knight comes into your life like a whirlwind, and you will have no doubt about his feelings for you. In general, this card may predict the arrival of a visitor.

REVERSED: Progress stops and interest falters. The reversed Knight may represent an individual who has a habit of rushing headlong into new relationships, causing arguments and chaos, then leaving as quickly as he arrived. It is best not to trust him.

50 THE MINOR ARCANA

QUEEN OF MOTHS

The Queen shows originality, intelligence, inspiring leadership, and communication. Passionate and creative, she loves nature and freedom, symbolized by the butterfly. All artistic pursuits and talk-based activities are favored. It is time to put your natural talents to work, or to appreciate others' artistic flair.

REVERSED: Poor management, miscommunication, and creative blocks are the indicators of the reversed Queen. As an individual, this person is resentful, hot-headed, and disruptive, and may be mean; avoid her influence.

KING OF MOTHS

This King brings you trust, friendship, and compassion. Talkative and inspirational, he is often a leader or an educator with an engaging personality who connects naturally with people. This is also the card of the artist, so artistic pursuits are favored now. As a potential partner, the King of Moths will make his feelings known.

REVERSED: There is an air of mistrust or prejudice as a once-happy situation becomes quite the reverse. As an individual, this King may be overbearing, intolerant, and full of self-interest. It may be better to accept this situation and look elsewhere than try to negotiate.

THE MINOR ARCANA 51

THE SUIT OF BEES

THE ELEMENT OF AIR

TRADITIONAL TAROT SUIT OF SWORDS

ACE OF BEES

The Ace brings the gift of victory, and this Bee offers a diamond, a symbol of purity, commitment, and energy. As Bees are the element of Air, the suit of the mind, this success is due to focus and clarity of thought—your win is well deserved and even hard-won, and may have involved intense work. However the Ace honors you, in victory you shine.

Reversed: This card represents thwarted success and a lost opportunity as a project fails or falters. However, it's not too late to try again—so rewind and make a plan. Channel your energy into your restart, rather than give in to frustration.

TWO OF BEES

The Two shows a difficult negotiation. Success is possible, but there seems to be no leeway right now as you reach stalemate. This card can show up when a relationship or other path to happiness is temporarily blocked. Listen to your head rather than your heart.

Reversed: Everything has stopped due to stubbornness or even deception and there is no clear reason why you should be in this position. Open your eyes to the truth and you may see the reason for the problem you face.

THREE OF BEES

This is a time of sorrow, loss, and even betrayal. The Three of Bees can indicate a breakup, as well as intense stress—the kind that strikes at your heart—in other areas of your life. This card may also represent three people in conflict. Painful and unexpected though it is, the wound left by your loss will heal.

REVERSED: The reversed Three of Bees indicates anxiety about a recent loss. The situation of the upright Three has passed, and it is time to recover from disappointment or shock. Don't let a testing situation worsen by taking the blame.

FOUR OF BEES

The Four can indicate a welcome rest after exertion and recuperation after illness or hospitalization. However, in relationships and projects, it represents a "limbo" state, during which there is very little energy or action. This can be positive, as it gives you time for recovery and reflection. An additional meaning is that a romance is put on hold.

REVERSED: Illness or unnecessary delays to projects may force you to take time away from everyday life. As this is not your choice, you may feel frustrated and isolated until you have at least a clearer picture of the future.

FIVE OF BEES

The Five shows anger, conflict, and failure. A fight creates tension and division, and you are the one who must pick up the pieces—and put yourself back together. There is little point in prolonging a losing battle or waging new wars. Others have strong opinions and may not consider your position. It is best to retreat.

REVERSED: The reversed meaning is similar to this card's upright meaning: You are surrounded by people who don't support you and who are more interested in competing. It is better to admit to making a mistake rather than give others fuel for their spite.

SIX OF BEES

It's time to take flight. This is often a welcome card, as it shows change and transition ahead as you travel physically and/or emotionally to a calmer space from which you can welcome new, uplifting experiences. The Six also shows that problems will dissolve and order will return. You can now enjoy distance and perspective.

REVERSED: In this position, you may need to leave your present situation, but can't see a way to do this just now. You may have tried and failed in the past. Making a change is all about timing—pick your time, keep focused, and you'll soon succeed.

SEVEN OF BEES

The Seven shows a lack of trust as you sense that something may be taken from you. Rather than appreciate your hard-won progress, you must spend precious time and energy protecting yourself from a devious opponent. On a mundane level, this card asks you to guard your possessions and beware of insincerity.

REVERSED: When reversed, this unsettling card shows more intense pressure from an antagonist whom you choose not to fight. You can confront them rather than let them have their own way—you may be cunning and strategic, too.

EIGHT OF BEES

This is the card that represents restriction. You may feel trapped and at the mercy of others. Overthinking may also be causing anxiety, so this card can relate to negative thought patterns and not being able to speak your truth or see a way out. Equally, a relationship or career path may have hit a block. Invite others to give you rational advice.

REVERSED: The reversed Eight brings adversity that is difficult to endure because you may feel victimized. What counts is how you adapt to your circumstances. Rather than vent frustration, calmly look at your options.

NINE OF BEES

The Nine denotes a period of stress. You may feel vulnerable, be under intense pressure, or feel unfairly treated, which leaves you with anxious, runaway thoughts. This Nine can also show disturbed dreams, signified by the moon, planet of the subconscious. Take heart, as this stressful time will pass.

REVERSED: The reversed Nine is a more acute expression of the upright card. You may feel despair or guilt, caught up in a cycle of negative thinking. Ask for help, so that when life gets a little easier, you will notice the difference—and break the pattern.

TEN OF BEES

The Ten, as the culmination of the forceful suit of Bees, shows dramatic endings; it is a common card for betrayal, redundancy, or the end of a relationship or friendship. There is failure and a situation that cannot go any further. This is unavoidable but at least it is finite, and it is now clear that you must move on. You can do it.

REVERSED: When reversed, the meaning is the same as that of the upright card, but here there is false hope and avoidance. Yet when you look at people's actions, there is no doubt they have made their feelings known. It is better to face the truth.

PAGE OF BEES

Challenges may lie ahead, so it pays to be sharp and single-minded; keep your wits about you.
A contract or other legal issue may need your attention. As a person, the Page is a clever advocate who is good with words and can turn negatives into positives. Intelligent and charming, he often brings news.

REVERSED: Expect delays with legal issues. Maliciousness and even lies may lead to an uncomfortable atmosphere. As a person, the reversed Page brings gossip and interference. Double-check all documents and arrangements.

KNIGHT OF BEES

Tension is brewing and battles are coming. Conflict, challenges, and opponents gather, and you need to quickly confront these blocks to your progress. Thankfully, the sting is swift. As a symbol of a person, the Knight is quick-witted, charming, and ruthless; he is a brilliant ally but a formidable opponent. There may be a price to pay to have him on your side.

REVERSED: With such unnecessary conflict and egomania around you, you may find yourself caught up in a negative situation over which you have little control. The reversed Knight represents a person who displays false heroics and even cowardice—don't rely upon him to stand by you.

QUEEN OF BEES

This Queen represents determination, charm, and strong intuition. She is a good omen of success, particularly in business or in careers that require mental aptitude. As a person, she can be a lone woman who is tough, independent, and brave, shown by her metal heart. She is Queen Bee of her hive, and her needs usually come first.

REVERSED: There may be manipulation and mistrust. The reversed Queen can be obsessive; she makes a virtue out of her failings. Try to avoid her bitter, jealous sting.

KING OF BEES

This King heralds a time for action, common sense, and problem-solving. He can represent the positive influence of a professional man, such as a lawyer or business leader who is clever, witty, and ambitious. He sees the big picture and has energy, however he bores easily and may soon move on.

REVERSED: You may face great opposition. This reversed King is a destroyer, not a builder, and he will use cunning and necessary force to get his way. It is better to retreat now than waste time and energy defending yourself or your projects.

THE SUIT OF BEETLES

THE ELEMENT OF EARTH

TRADITIONAL TAROT SUIT OF PENTACLES OR COINS

ACE OF BEETLES

This Ace brings the gifts of money and success. The Beetle holds a piece of amber, a symbol of abundance, vitality, security, and the power of the sun. As the Beetle cards possess the elemental energy of supportive Mother Earth, so you may be offered an opportunity, reward, or gift. This is a wonderful, abundant time that favors new beginnings.

REVERSED: When reversed, this Ace shows money without responsibility or love. Here, money is a negative because it comes with conditions that go against your beliefs. You may also need to watch out for greed, within yourself or others.

TWO OF BEETLES

The two beetles, which appear with the lemniscate (figure-eight symbol), represent solvency, but it may be difficult to meet financial obligations and keep money flowing. This card may also highlight a personal dilemma. You are weighing up two options: places to live, a career path, or even a relationship. Don't ponder too long.

REVERSED: Loss and cash-flow problems are the messages of the reversed Two. Plans are halted or blocked due to issues with people. You may be so busy trying to get a grip on your finances or property, you fail to see that those around you are not giving enough.

THE MINOR ARCANA

THREE OF BEETLES

It is time to go out into the world. Your ideas take form, so creative pursuits, projects, and businesses are all favored now—you share your work with others and receive recognition for your craft. This card is a good omen for selling, interviews, and auditions. House moves and property renovations are additional meanings.

REVERSED: What you are trying to establish goes awry. This may be down to a lack of trust, or because you are avoiding essential details—the practicalities that make an idea work. It's time to begin again and to choose a path or project that can hold your attention.

FOUR OF BEETLES

Your efforts are rewarded with deserved success and security after a time of hard work. This card is reassurance that all will be well, and it is also auspicious for property, such as finding a new home. You are entering a phase during which money and security are important. An additional meaning of the Four is good health.

REVERSED: In reverse, this card represents struggle, frustration, and missed opportunities. There may be delays concerning property or debts to deal with. You may need to take a calculated risk to bring in money. Take heart that this start–stop phase will pass.

FIVE OF BEETLES

The traditional meaning of the Five is poverty and exclusion, although this is usually a fear of poverty or feeling alone, rather than a reality. Money may be tight, but you have more resources than you realize—you just need to look further afield to find them. Problems will soon be solved.

REVERSED: You are experiencing poor money management, or there are arguments over material possessions. This not only isolates you, but affects your relationships, potentially leading to accusations and a lack of trust. Take another view and move on.

SIX OF BEETLES

The Six brings the spirit of generosity. You may give or receive money, but whatever your role— generous friend, mentor, or recipient—you will benefit. Life feels in balance as past problems are redressed. An unexpected gift may arrive in the form of a sum of money or a present you adore. Feel the love.

REVERSED: Money is withheld. Someone around you, or an institution, may be miserly or secretive about their finances, perhaps keeping back money and avoiding paying essential bills or personal debts. This meanness can cause only further ill feeling.

SEVEN OF BEETLES

Seven cards often show potential, and this Seven means that you are beginning to see the rewards of your dedication and hard work. You may not yet have achieved all your goals, but you are making good progress; keep up the effort and soon you will flourish. Don't think about what is missing. Focus on your success.

REVERSED: The reversed Seven shows unhappiness. You may be feeling shut down and deflated, but if you want success, you will need to keep taking action rather than accept the status quo; making a decision will give you energy. Also, take extreme care with money and other resources.

EIGHT OF BEETLES

Revealing patient hard work and its rewards, this Eight shows money coming to you and often shows the completion of an apprenticeship or other educational or professional course, leading to a fulfilling career or project. Value is also important now: value yourself and the skills you offer.

REVERSED: In reverse, this Eight can represent work without much enjoyment. Until you find an alternative, you may feel both trapped and frustrated. Try not to give all your time and energy to an employer, project, or relationship that you find so unrewarding.

NINE OF BEETLES

It is time to enjoy the finer things in life as you benefit from your investments, financially and emotionally. This is a time of security and protection, when you can indulge in a little luxury. You feel happy and content in your surroundings. This card can also show a helpful, financially independent woman.

REVERSED: The reversed Nine may highlight problems at home—general antagonism, or arguments about domestic arrangements and finances. Protect your money and property.

TEN OF BEETLES

The Ten shows the wealth of generations. As the last number card of the Beetles, it predicts ultimate wealth and material happiness. This is a time of security—money comes to you, and your family connections deepen and become more rewarding. This card may also represent a prosperous and happy marriage or business partnership.

REVERSED: Inheritance issues, financial stress, and family discord rule when the Ten reverses. Generations may clash; and money, or attitudes toward money and lifestyle get in the way of past love and harmony.

THE MINOR ARCANA 63

PAGE OF BEETLES

This Page brings good news about finances, and money matters take a turn for the better. While you don't receive everything you desire, there will be enough for you to further your plans. Look after the small money carefully and see it grow. As a person, the Page is methodical and hard working and very helpful to you.

REVERSED: Someone around you is taking an immature attitude and has delusions of grandeur—so take what they propose very lightly. This card can represent a younger person who must learn to organize their chaotic finances.

KNIGHT OF BEETLES

Little by little you are making progress. If you are waiting for money, you will receive it gradually. You may need to make consistent effort, so have patience. As symbol of a potential partner, the Knight is loyal and steadfast, but slow to show his feelings. He makes decisions in his own time, and you may have to do the running.

REVERSED: In reverse, this card represents financial misconduct. Before entering into an agreement, thoroughly check all of the details. As a person in your life, the reversed Knight can be stubborn and untrustworthy, with less to give than might first appear.

QUEEN OF BEETLES

The Queen's laurel wreath shows that she brings generosity and success to your affairs. She symbolizes order and good management. As a woman in your life, she appreciates material comfort and good business sense, and she is also kind, helpful, and down to earth—qualities that endear her to many. She knows how to look after her interests.

REVERSED: The reversed Queen can represent short-term money problems. As an individual, she shows extremes of temperament, veering from meanness to strange extravagances. She may try to buy your favor.

KING OF BEETLES

Solved problems, business success, and material comfort—what's not to like about this King? Fair and trustworthy, he signifies honest dealings and stable relationships. As a symbol of a potential partner, he is successful yet down to earth, which makes him attractive. He offers steady support along with financial security.

REVERSED: Corruption and money problems may arise when the King reverses. He predicts financial mismanagement, particularly concerning property. As an individual he is unforgiving and miserly; don't hope that he will change.

BIBLIOGRAPHY

Tarot Mysteries: *Rediscovering the Real Meanings of the Cards,* Jonathan Dee (Zambezi, 2003)
The Mystery of the Tarot: *Discover the Tarot and Find our What Your Cards Really Mean,* Liz Dean (CICO Books, 2003)